20TH CENTURY · DESIGN

1900-20

THE BIRTH OF MODERNISM

20TH CENTURY DESIGN – 1900-20
was produced by

David West 👫 Children's Books
7 Princeton Court
55 Felsham Road
London SW15 1AZ

Picture Research: Brooks Krikler Research

First published in Great Britain in 1999 by
Heinemann Library, Halley Court, Jordan Hill,
Oxford OX2 8EJ, a division of Reed Educational and
Professional Publishing Limited.

OXFORD MELBOURNE AUCKLAND
JOHANNESBURG BLANTYRE GABORONE
IBADAN PORTSMOUTH (NH) USA CHICAGO

Copyright © 1999 David West Children's Books

03 02 01 00 99
10 9 8 7 6 5 4 3 2 1

ISBN 0 431 03950 X (HB)
ISBN 0 431 03951 8 (PB)

British Library Cataloguing in Publication Data

Gaff, Jackie
Birth of modernism (1900 - 1920). - (Design in the
twentieth century)
1. Design - History - 20th century - Juvenile literature
I. Title
745.4'442

Printed and bound in Italy

PHOTO CREDITS :
Abbreviations: t-top, m-middle, b-bottom,
r-right, l-left, c-centre.

Front cover & 7t - Frank Spooner
Pictures. Cover tr & mc, 3mr, 4-5b, 5l, 8
both, 9 both, 10b, 11t, 12t & m, 13, 14t
& m, 15tl & tr, 16bl, 18 all, 19bl, 20bl,
24-25 & 25t - Corbis. Cover ml & bl, 7b,
8-9, 10t, 11br, 12b, 15b, 16t & br, 19tr
& br, 20br, 21tl, 24bl & 29b - AKG
London. Cover, 4-5t, 26m & bl & br -
Solution Pictures. 4m - Tom Donovan
Military Pictures. 5r & 22m - UPI/Corbis.
5 & 17b - Vitra Design Museum. 6tl &
11bl - Roger Viollet Collection/Frank
Spooner Pictures. 6tr, 6-7, 21tr, 22t & b,
24t, 25b & 29t - Mary Evans Picture
Library. 14b & 17t - © Hunterian Art
Gallery, University of Glasgow,
Mackintosh Collection. 23t -
Corbis/Bettmann. 23b - Hulton Getty
Collection. 26tr & 27 both - Philip
Jarrett. 28l - AKG: Peter Behrens©DACS
1999. 28r - Reproduced by kind
permission of the London Transport
Museum.

*The dates in brackets after a designer's
name give the years that he or she lived.
Where a date appears after an object (or, in
the case of a building, the town where it is
situated), it is the year of its design.
'C.' stands for circa, meaning about or
approximately.*

*An explanation of difficult words can be
found in the glossary on page 30.*

20TH CENTURY · DESIGN

1900-20
THE BIRTH OF MODERNISM

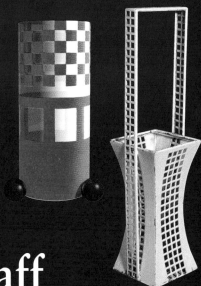

Jackie Gaff

Heinemann
LIBRARY

CONTENTS

The invention of the petrol engine in the 19th century made powered flight possible in the 20th – the first-ever powered plane, the Wright brothers' Flyer, took off in 1903.

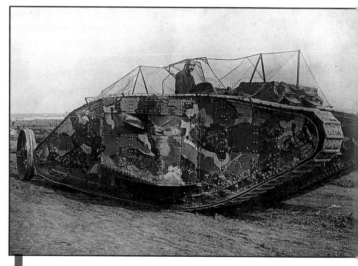

The first armoured tanks went into battle in 1916. Territorial disputes had led to the outbreak of World War I in 1914. By the time peace was declared in 1918, around 8 million troops had been killed.

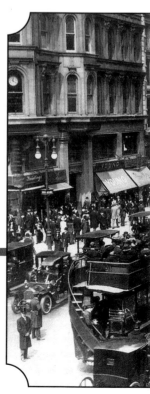

It is often many years before 'old' technology is replaced by the new. Even by 1915, horse-drawn carriages were still a common sight on the streets of New York.

THE NEW CENTURY

Change rarely happens overnight, and the first two decades of the 20th century saw the old gradually giving way to the new. The 19th century had seen many remarkable inventions – including the electric motor and the petrol engine – but only now, as better mass-production techniques brought lower prices, did the new products begin to touch ordinary people's lives.

A new equality was also forged during the horror of World War I (1914–18). While men from all walks of life fought side-by-side in the mud of the trenches, women took up their jobs at home and tasted new financial and social freedoms.

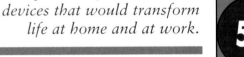

The graceful curves of art nouveau style were all the rage in 1900 (electric lamp by Louis Comfort Tiffany).

The new century brought an explosion of new electrical devices that would transform life at home and at work.

In art and architecture, the year 1900 saw the ornate curves and stylized, natural imagery of art nouveau style at the height of their popularity. By 1920, an artistic revolution had taken place – radical artists, architects and designers had turned away from the world of nature and found new inspiration in the exploration of abstract, geometric forms.

By 1920, a less decorative, abstract style had emerged (Red and Blue armchair, Gerrit Rietveld, 1918).

FASHIONABLE FINERY

The first few years of the new century saw little change in the formal rigidity of middle-class fashion. Men and women had to wear the correct outfit for morning, afternoon and evening, and had a range of costumes which were designed specifically for activities such as walking or riding in the new motorcars.

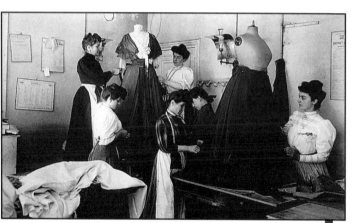

Sewing machines were a 19th-century invention, but most clothes were still handmade.

This woman's curvy, 'S-bend' figure and elegant walking costume were the height of fashion in the early 1900s.

VISIONS OF LOVELINESS

Fashionable women were fantasies of soft and submissive femininity, swathed in rustling chiffon and lace. Necklines were low for evening, but skirts were long and full to prevent a shocking glimpse of ankle or calf.

UNDERCOVER STORY

Beneath this fragile exterior, beating hearts were restrained by layers of elaborate undergarments and a heavily-boned corset. The fashionable female silhouette, the S-bend, was achieved by a tightly-laced corset that thrust out the bottom, pulled in the waist and pushed out the bust.

Women's dresses (and underwear) began to loosen up a little towards 1910. This painting is of a ball held at London's Savoy Hotel in 1912.

THE WINDS OF CHANGE

Women in New Zealand and three American states had achieved the vote back in the 1890s, and suffragettes were campaigning to extend this right to all women. Freedom was in the air – a few radical women had abandoned corsets for unboned stays during the 19th century, and by 1910 a straighter silhouette was coming into vogue. These more relaxed fashions were greatly influenced by the exotic, oriental-style costumes and sets designed by Léon Bakst (1866–1924) for the Russian Ballet. The company had caused a sensation when they first performed in Paris in 1909.

Poiret's 1911–13 collections featured these pantaloon dresses. The central one has a 'lampshade' over-tunic.

PAUL POIRET'S LIBERATED LOOK

If any one person was responsible for loosening up women's fashions, it was the French couturier Paul Poiret (1879–1944). In 1906, he launched a simple, loose, high-waisted dress, while his 1909 collection featured harem pants inspired by the Russian Ballet. His 'lampshade' tunic followed in 1911.

WEARING THE TROUSERS

War work called for functional clothing, and for the first time it became acceptable for Western women to wear trousers. Jodhpurs were considered practical for farmwork, and boiler suits for some factory jobs. The experience was to change attitudes to women and clothing forever.

Not all of Poiret's designs were liberating. His 'hobble skirt' of 1911 was so narrow at the ankle that the wearer could only manage tiny steps.

ART NOUVEAU

The words *art nouveau* are French for 'new art', and the style developed in the 1880s in reaction to the prevailing fashion for historical or 'old' styles. For much of the 19th century, artists and architects had looked back to the art and design of the past for inspiration. But with the approach of the new century, some people began to look forwards and to develop modern styles for the modern age.

LEARNING THE LINES

The use of line was at the heart of art nouveau style – it was long, sinuous (or winding) and flowing, with a sense of lightness and grace. Images were drawn mainly from the natural world, and ranged from curling vine tendrils and twisting locks of human hair, to peacocks, dragonflies, snakes, greyhounds, bats, irises, orchids and lilies.

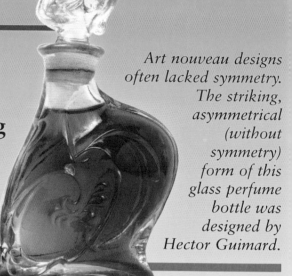

Art nouveau designs often lacked symmetry. The striking, asymmetrical (without symmetry) form of this glass perfume bottle was designed by Hector Guimard.

The swirling, stylized art-work of the Czech painter Alphonse Mucha (1860–1939) is the epitome of art nouveau style (poster for Job cigarettes, 1898).

FANNING THE FLAMES

Art nouveau spread like wildfire, promoted by international exhibitions and new art journals such as *The Studio* (launched in 1893). Distinctive interpretations of the style developed in different cities, with the main centres being Paris and Nancy in France, Munich, Berlin and Darmstadt in Germany, Brussels in Belgium, Barcelona in Spain, Glasgow in Scotland, Vienna in Austria, and New York and Chicago in the United States. In Germany, it was known as *Jugendstil* (or 'young style') after the *Jugend* magazine.

SIMPLIFYING THE LOOK

As art nouveau matured, a new style evolved. The sinuous, curving line remained popular well into the early 1900s, and was seen in the work of designers such as the Parisian Hector Guimard (1867–1942) and the Barcelonan Antonio Gaudí (1852–1926). However, inspired by the Glaswegian Charles Rennie Mackintosh (1868–1928), other designers began to explore straight lines and geometric forms.

The Belgian architect and designer Henry van de Velde (1863–1957) rejected plant and animal motifs and explored abstract, curving patterns (stained-glass windows, late 1890s).

The French architect and designer Hector Guimard is best-known for the fantastical, sinuous, plant-like forms he created for the Paris underground system, the Métro (begun in 1903).

GLASS MASTERS

Light, airy and delicate, glass was an ideal art nouveau material. Master craftsmen such as Frenchman Emile Gallé (1846–1904) and American Louis Comfort Tiffany (1848–1933) experimented with glass-making techniques to create ethereally beautiful pieces of sculpture. Gallé opened his own glassworks in Nancy, France, in 1874, while Tiffany opened his workshops on Long Island, New York, in 1893. Many of Tiffany's pieces glow with an iridescent metallic finish, achieved by spraying on metallic vapours.

Tiffany also created magical lampshades out of stained glass (Poppy table lamp, with bronze base).

THE NEW ARCHITECTURE

Architects were at the forefront of the movement to create new styles for the modern age, and the 1890s and early 1900s saw a flowering of astonishing art nouveau buildings in cities throughout Europe. And it wasn't only the look of these buildings that was novel, but the way that they were constructed.

Like Charles Rennie Mackintosh, Josef Hoffmann explored abstract, geometric forms in his work (Palais Stoclet, Brussels, 1905–11).

INDUSTRIAL MATERIALS

Techniques for mass-producing cast and wrought iron had been developed in the 19th century, and iron had been used to magnificent effect by the engineers responsible for constructing public buildings such as railway stations. But although it could provide a strong and comparatively light framework, architects had been slow to use iron, and even when they did it was usually hidden behind brick and stonework. Many art nouveau architects were excited by the decorative potential of cast and wrought iron, however, and they not only used it in the construction of their buildings, they often left it exposed to view.

The clean lines and stark pebbledash exterior of Charles Rennie Mackintosh's Hill House looked electrifyingly modern in the early 1900s (Helensburgh, near Glasgow, 1902–03).

LONE GENIUS

The American Frank Lloyd Wright (1857–1959) was one of the 20th century's most innovative architects and his work had enormous impact on architecture worldwide. He avoided current styles and pursued his own personal vision throughout his long career. Wright had a great love of natural materials such as wood and said that he aimed to build 'organic architecture' – buildings that seemed to grow naturally from the landscape.

Frank Lloyd Wright became well known in the early 1900s for his Prairie Houses – homes with low horizontal exteriors, projecting roofs, and open-plan interiors (Frederick C. Robie House, Chicago, 1909).

DECORATIVE IRONWORK

One of the first art nouveau architects to do this was the Belgian Victor Horta (1861–1947), who exposed the internal iron columns that carried much of the weight of his Hôtel Tassel (Brussels, 1892). Not only did he not cover the columns, he moulded them into fantastical plant stems complete with twisting fronds.

Antonio Gaudí once said that there are no straight lines in nature, and his undulating Casa Batlló looks more like a lizard than an apartment block (Barcelona, 1904–06)!

Decorative ironwork was also used for the windows of Victor Horta's Hôtel Tassel.

TREND SPOTTING

Horta and the extraordinary Spaniard Antonio Gaudí were two of the architects to develop the more sinuous style of art nouveau. Others such as Scotland's Charles Rennie Mackintosh and the Austrian Josef Hoffmann (1870–1956) evolved a less ornate style, using straight, horizontal and vertical lines. The great American architect Frank Lloyd Wright was just as passionate about straight lines, but his work was so individual that it is not usually considered part of the art nouveau movement.

ART & INDUSTRY

The development of industrial manufacturing during the 1800s had brought with it a flood of poorly designed products, and the last decades of the century saw a growing revolt against this.

Italian engineer Matté Truco's Lingotto car factory for Fiat was a masterpiece of reinforced-concrete construction (Turin, 1915).

QUALITY CONTROL

For some architects and designers, this revolt meant a return to handcrafted goods in natural materials such as wood. But for others it meant forging closer links between art and industry, and the creation of well-designed products which made the most of modern technology and modern materials such as reinforced concrete and steel. And, of course, some people were interested in doing both!

GROUP WORK

Several organizations formed to promote these ideas, including the Vienna Workshops and the Deutsche Werkbund (German work association) which was founded in 1907 to unite business and industry with the arts and crafts. One of its co-founders was the German architect and designer Peter Behrens (1868–1940), who was among the first to design specifically for industry.

The box-like Fagus shoe factory is one of the earliest examples of the modernist style that flourished after World War I. It was designed in 1910 by the German-born architects Walter Gropius (1883–1969) and Adolf Meyer (1881–1929).

Peter Behrens created this starkly simple design for the AEG's turbine factory in 1908–09.

DESIGNING FOR INDUSTRY

Behrens had been working mainly with handcrafted goods until 1907, when he was appointed design consultant to the German electrical company AEG and began styling its publications, products and factories. Gradually, through the work of designers such as Behrens, there was a shift away from the nature-inspired imagery of art nouveau towards simple, undecorated, geometrical buildings and objects. These were not only the products of the modern age, they seemed to symbolize it, and by the '30s the style had come to be known as modernism.

THE AMERICAN REVOLUTION

Buildings were up to 400 metres high in the United States by the 1880s, but construction methods made it impossible to go higher. In Chicago in '83, architect William Jenney (1832–1907) designed a building in which the weight was carried by a metal framework instead of load-bearing walls (the Home Insurance Building). Mass-production of steel had been developed in Britain, the United States and Germany in the 1850s–70s. The first building with an all-steel skeleton was also built in Chicago (the Tacoma Building, '87–88).

Steel-girder skeleton

Non load-bearing walls

In Chicago, architects explored the design possibilities of the skyscraper, using strong, vertical lines and large windows (Reliance Building, Chicago (1890–94).

13

INDOOR STYLE

Victorian rooms had been cluttered and gloomy, with furniture and windows swathed in heavy, elaborate fabrics, and bold, dark colour schemes. Art nouveau interiors were completely the opposite – simple, spacious and filled with light. The change was largely due to the new approach taken by architects in the late 19th century.

Frank Lloyd Wright pioneered the removal of internal walls to create open-plan interiors, and created rooms that flowed naturally out into the landscape (Hollyhock House, Los Angeles, 1918).

A TOTAL LOOK

No longer content with designing just the structure and exterior of a building, architects began to style every aspect of the interior, from the colour of the walls, to the shape of chairs and door handles. A building and its contents became a single, harmonized work of art. 'It is quite impossible to consider the building as one thing, its furnishings another and its setting and environment still another,' wrote the American architect Frank Lloyd Wright.

Usually Charles Rennie Mackintosh worked with his designer wife Margaret Macdonald on fittings such as these doors (Willow Tea Rooms, Glasgow, 1903–05).

In 1906, the Mackintoshes designed simple, light-filled, white interiors for their own home in Glasgow.

In 1905–06, Frank Lloyd Wright designed the Unity Temple church, styling every corner of its interior, including these sculptural electric lights (Oak Park, Chicago).

Like Lloyd Wright, the American Greene brothers, Charles (1868–1957) and Henry (1870–1954), created light, open-plan interiors and liked to work with local materials, particularly wood (kitchen of the Gamble House, California, 1907–08).

LETTING IN THE LIGHT

Art nouveau architects flooded rooms with light, increasing the size of windows and using skylights and the new electric lights invented in the 1870s. Stained-glass panels filtered daylight into softly glowing colours, while walls were painted in white or delicate shades of grey, olive and mauve – a shade that technology had only recently made available. For thousands of years, dyes had been made from natural materials – purple had been obtained from shellfish since 1500 BC, for example, but this had made it so rare that it was reserved for royalty. The first synthetic dye, mauveine, was discovered by the British chemist Sir William Perkin (1838–1907). Although he began making the dye in 1856, it did not become fashionable until the '90s.

The extraordinary Antonio Gaudí turned the inside of his Casa Milá into an underwater grotto (Barcelona, 1905–10).

FURNITURE

Art nouveau architects not only gave the exterior of their buildings sinuous curves, but designed interiors to match. The most excessive pieces of art nouveau furniture looked like flowering bushes, with their feet turned into roots, and their framework carved into the trunk and branches crowned with blossoming flowers.

The Belgian architect Victor Horta designed his own Brussels home in 1898–1901, and every last object swirls with elegant art nouveau style.

16

CREATING A TOTAL LOOK

Beetles, dragonflies and other insects were favourite decorative motifs, while the wildly inventive Italian designer and furniture maker Carlo Bugatti (1856–1940) created an entire Snail Room! The idea of designing everything in a room to give it a total look was an early 20th century innovation.

In the past, various styles had been jumbled up together without a common theme.

The designs of Italy's Carlo Bugatti equalled Spain's Antonio Gaudí's in eccentricity. This bizarre creation is a wooden cabinet!

The most distinctive thing about Charles Rennie Mackintosh's chairs is the strong vertical line of their extremely high backs (1906).

LEADING LIGHTS

Great French furniture designers of the period included Emile Gallé and Louis Majorelle (1859–1926), while in Belgium the field was led by Victor Horta and Henry van de Velde. Van de Velde had moved to a less decorative art nouveau style by the early 1900s, with a simpler use of line and form. He had come to believe that an object should no longer reflect the external world of nature, and that true beauty lay in usefulness rather than decoration.

CLEANING UP THE ACT

Perhaps the most influential person in the trend towards simplification was Scotland's Charles Rennie Mackintosh. His furniture was plain to the point of severity, and often very uncomfortable – unlike van de Velde, Mackintosh was more concerned with shape than with usefulness or function.

By the early 1900s, Henry van de Velde's furniture designs were simple and functional. He was one of the founders of the Deutsche Werkbund.

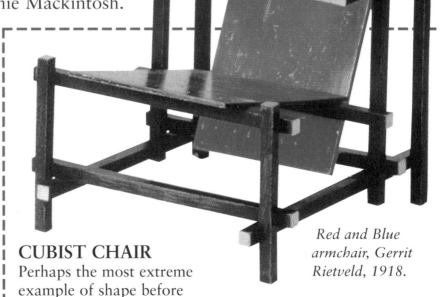

Red and Blue armchair, Gerrit Rietveld, 1918.

CUBIST CHAIR

Perhaps the most extreme example of shape before comfort was created by the Dutchman Gerrit Rietveld (1888–1964). Architects and designers were part of a far wider art movement, and Rietveld's chair reflects the interest in primary colours and geometric shapes being explored by cubist painters such as Piet Mondrian (1872–1944).

THE VIENNA WORKSHOPS

The Vienna Workshops (or Wiener Werkstätte) was an association of more than 90 artists and craftworkers which was founded in 1903 by the architect and designer Josef Hoffmann and the painter Koloman Moser (1868–1918). Hoffmann said that the Workshops' aim was to develop 'an intimate relationship between the public, the designer and the craftsman, and to create good, simple things for the home'.

This 1917 poster for the Workshops' fashions was designed by one of the group's leading members, Dagobert Peche (1887–1923).

The fashion studios created accessories, fabrics and clothes (handbag c. 1910).

18

DESIGN STUDIOS

The Vienna Workshops consisted of a number of small studios which produced expensive, high-quality, handcrafted goods in luxury materials. Different studios specialized in different fields, including furniture, metalwork, glassware, ceramics (or pottery), bookbinding, jewellery and, from 1910, clothes and fashion accessories. Like many other people at the time, members of the group rejected historical styles and sought to create new ones. Hoffmann had invited Charles Rennie Mackintosh to Vienna in 1900, and the group's early designs were greatly influenced by Mackintosh's less ornate, more geometric style.

The Workshops left no corner of the home unstyled! This child's wooden toy town dates from about 1918.

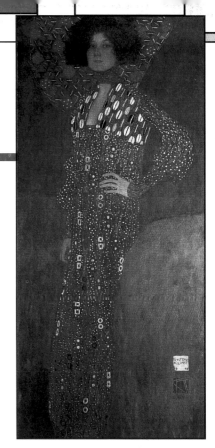

The Austrian painter Gustav Klimt (1862–1918) had close connections with the Vienna Workshops, and helped with fashion designs and by creating mosaic wall murals. He also painted portraits of some of the Workshop members (portrait of Miss Emilie Floege, 1902).

ARTS & CRAFTS MOVEMENT

The Vienna Workshops was one of a number of associations inspired by the English arts and crafts movement of the mid-1850s. Led by idealists such as the poet William Morris (1834–96), the movement opposed mass-production and sought instead to revive the importance of craftsmanship.

Geometric checks were a favourite motif in the Workshops' early years (vase by Jutta Sika, c. 1905).

MASS MARKET DESIGN

The movement also believed that well-designed, well-crafted goods should be available to all. Only the wealthy could afford the Workshops' handmade goods, though, and this aim was not realized until people like Peter Behrens (who had also been a member of an arts and crafts group in the early 1900s) began designing for mass-production.

The severity of this metallic basket was intended to be softened by a pot plant (Josef Hoffmann, c. 1905).

STYLE SETTER
Like many architects of the time, Josef Hoffmann was interested in all aspects of design, styling everything from furniture and glassware to carpets and cutlery. He did not draw upon the natural world for imagery, and his focus on geometrical shapes earned him the nickname *Quadratl* or 'Little Square'. Hoffmann's work influenced the purely geometric styles of the 1920s and '30s.

Hoffmann liked to contrast his use of line with circular motifs and real plants (sketch for an interior, 1899).

TURNING THE TABLES

As with the furniture designs of the early 20th century, the styling of glass and other tableware ranged from the ornate art nouveau of Louis Comfort Tiffany, to the more restrained, geometric patterns of Josef Hoffmann and the Vienna Workshops. And while some people focussed on handcrafted objects, others began to design deliberately for mass-production.

THE STORY OF GLASS

Technological developments helped to revolutionize the production of glassware, in particular. Since its invention in the Middle East in about 100 BC, the art of glass-blowing had involved a human glass-maker blowing air down a narrow metal tube into a lump of molten glass. The technique remained unchanged until the late 19th century, when people began to experiment with using machine-compressed air instead of blowing by mouth.

Frank Lloyd Wright also explored abstract forms. He designed this porcelain plate setting for the Imperial Hotel, Tokyo, in 1915–22.

Designers such as Josef Hoffmann continued to create objects to be handmade by craftworkers. The decoration on this delicate glassware was handpainted (c. 1912).

Swirling colours and shapes such as these could never be achieved by a machine (Louis Comfort Tiffany, Jack-in-the-Pulpit vase, c. 1912).

20

MACHINES TAKE OVER

By 1907, bottles and other glass containers were being made automatically, with machines doing everything from mixing and firing the raw materials, to moulding and shaping the bottle, and the final annealing (or heat treatment). Production rates rose to 2,500 bottles an hour (from 200 bottles an hour in the 1880s), and prices dropped. Similar developments were also taking place in other industries, making low-cost, functional tableware more widely available.

NEW MATERIALS

It wasn't just production methods that were changing, though – new materials were also being introduced. The first stainless steel knives were made in Sheffield in 1914 for the British scientist Harold Brearley (1871–1948). Stainless steel is very resistant to rusting, and Brearley had realized its commercial potential when investigating its use for rifle barrels.

The Coca-Cola bottle is probably the world's most famous piece of packaging. The drink was invented in 1886, and the bottle was given its shape in 1915–20.

New on the table in 1915 was the heat-resistant glassware marketed by the American company Pyrex Corning.

21

TURNING BOTTLE-MAKING ON ITS HEAD

In automatic glass-making, molten glass flows into a mould that has the bottle's neck and mouth at its base. Compressed air is blown in, and this pushes the molten glass up into the mould to form a thick-walled bottle called a blank. The blank is turned the correct way up and put in a finishing mould, where compressed air is used to blow the final shape.

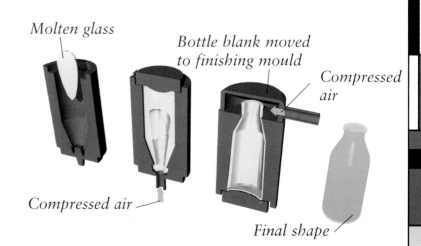

Molten glass

Bottle blank moved to finishing mould

Compressed air

Compressed air

Final shape

NNOVATIONS AT HOME

The technological development that had the greatest impact on home life in the early 20th century was the introduction of electric power. The first power stations had begun operating in the 1880s, but for the next few decades only the wealthy could afford to have electricity supplied to their homes. This did not prevent a flood of new electrical devices, though.

THE FIRST DUST-BUSTERS

The first vacuum cleaner was patented in 1901 by the British engineer Hubert Booth (1871–1955). Booth's machine was powered by a petrol engine and it sucked dust down long hoses to a horse-drawn cart parked outside the house. Portable electric vacuum cleaners were developed in the United States, and the first was marketed in 1908 by William Hoover (1849–1932).

Power connections could be unusual in the early days of electricity. This 1913 teamaker is plugged into a light socket!

The first people to benefit from new electrical devices like this floor polisher were wealthy families' servants.

Early electrical devices were expensive, but mass-production brought rapid price reductions. By the '30s, hoovers cost a third less than they did in 1920.

The New HOOVER
It BEATS ... as it Sweeps ... as it Cleans

By Appointment

The HOOVER

more d.p.m.
— DIRT PER MINUTE —
The accurate measure of electric cleaner efficiency

This electric kettle was designed by Peter Behrens for the German AEG company in 1909.

An easy way to shop for household goods was to order them from a mail order firm. In the United States, Sears Roebuck had mailed their first catalogue in 1896.

PRIVATE HOMES

Most 19th-century households, apart from those of the very poor, had relied on at least one live-in servant – and often a whole army of them – to do the cooking, cleaning, washing and ironing by hand. But by the 1910s, the choice of jobs had widened and fewer people were choosing to go into domestic service. As servants became less and less available, labour-saving electrical devices like the vacuum cleaner filled the gap. And without live-in servants, the home evolved into a private space for the family.

Edison's phonograph could record and replay, so you could either buy cylinders or create your own.

23

MUSICAL MACHINES

Two kinds of record player were available in the 1900s – the phonograph invented by Thomas Edison (1847–1931) in 1877, and the gramophone trade-marked by Emil Berliner (1851–1929) in 1894. Edison's phonograph used cylinders coated in tinfoil or wax, while Berliner's gramophone was the first to use a flat disc (or record) made from shellac (a natural plastic resin secreted by the lac insect). By 1920, records had virtually replaced cylinders.

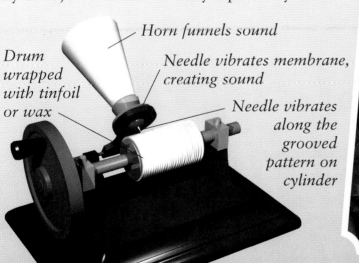

Horn funnels sound

Drum wrapped with tinfoil or wax

Needle vibrates membrane, creating sound

Needle vibrates along the grooved pattern on cylinder

TRANSPORT

Before 1900 ordinary people travelled by horse, bicycle, boat and train, but most often on their own two feet. The new century opened the door to other methods of transport, with bus, tram and underground train networks branching out into the suburbs of every major city.

CHANGE OF POWER

A steam locomotive had pulled the first underground train in London in 1863, and it wasn't until the first electric locomotive was demonstrated in Berlin in '79 that modern electric tram and railway systems became possible. It took time to catch up with the new technology, and underground systems only began to be built in Europe and the United States in the late '90s. The other great 19th century invention was, of course, the petrol-driven car. The first ones were made by the German engineers Karl Benz (1844–1929) in '85 and Gottlieb Daimler (1834–1900) in '86.

24

"Griffon"

All the early motorcycles were built by their inventors and not sold to the public. The first motorcycle factory opened in Germany in 1894, and the bike in this poster dates from 1905.

Early motorcars had no roofs, doors or windscreens, so passengers had to cover themselves from head to toe to keep off the dust and rain.

CUTTING THE COSTS

For many years, cars were so expensive to manufacture that only the wealthy could afford them. Mass-production of cars began in the United States in 1901, when it was pioneered by the Oldsmobile Company. It was further developed by the engineer Henry Ford (1863–1947), who founded his own car manufacturing company in Detroit in 1903.

MOTORCARS FOR THE MASSES

Ford aimed to build a car 'so low in price that no man making a good salary will be unable to own one', and in 1908 he launched his affordable Model T Ford. His major breakthrough in reducing costs came in '13, when he introduced the moving assembly line to his factories. This reduced the time taken to produce the chassis of a Model T Ford from 728 to 93 minutes!

Even in big cities like New York, it was a long time before the motorcar replaced the horse-drawn carriage – this busy street scene dates from 1915.

PUTTING THE PARTS TOGETHER

Ford's assembly line made manufacturing faster and more efficient by breaking the process down into a series of tasks, each one carried out by a different person or machine. The car was forwarded to each work station on a moving conveyor belt.

Ford's first cars rolled off his assembly line in 1913.

LOSS OF A TITAN

The *Titanic* was the largest and most luxurious ocean liner ever built, and believed to be the safest until it struck an iceberg on 14th April 1912. This was the greatest transport disaster the world had ever known – more than 1,500 people perished.

The Titanic sank within three hours of hitting an iceberg.

FLYING MACHINES

The petrol engine not only transformed land transport, it opened up the skies to powered flying machines. Daring aviators had experimented with gliders and hang-gliders during the 19th century, but there had been one big stumbling block to powered flight – the lack of a suitable engine.

THE BIG DAY DAWNS

The first successful flight of a powered aircraft took place at Kitty Hawk, North Carolina, the United States, on a frosty morning in December 1903. The plane was called *Flyer*, and its rather bumpy maiden flight lasted for 12 seconds. This historic event was the work of the two Wright brothers, Orville (1871–1948) and Wilbur (1867–1912). Their research had involved testing full-sized gliders in a home-built wind-tunnel and making more than 1,000 glider flights. The brothers had found car engines too heavy, and their final achievement was designing and building their own lightweight plane engine.

The Flyer's *lightweight engine was mounted on the plane's lower wing.*

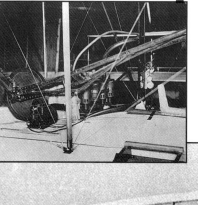

26

Flyer *carried one pilot, lying face down beside the engine. The brothers tossed a coin to decide who flew first – Orville won the toss.*

The Wright brothers designed and made bicycles before becoming fascinated by flight in the 1890s.

Alcock and Brown took 16 hours and 12 minutes to fly across the Atlantic on June 14–15 1919, winning fame, glory – and £10,000 from a newspaper!

RECORD-BREAKING DECADES

The next 30 years saw one flying record being broken after another, as engineers raced to build better and faster machines. In 1909 Frenchman Louis Blériot became the first person to fly across the English Channel, and in 1919 British pilots John Alcock and Arthur Brown made the first non-stop transatlantic flight.

MATERIAL GAINS

All these records went hand-in-hand with technological advances, and the next big breakthrough came in the materials used for aircraft construction. The first planes had largely been made from wood and canvas, and it was not until 1919 that practical, all-metal aircraft were built. This was made possible by the development in 1908–12 of a lightweight aluminium alloy called duralumin.

Commercial passenger flights started taking off in 1919 – in converted wartime bombers.

POSITIVE BENEFITS OF PURE ALUMINIUM

Producing aluminium alloys in commercial quantities had been made possible by the invention in the 1880s of a technique for using electrolysis to obtain pure aluminium from alumina (aluminium oxide). Molten alumina and cryolite (another aluminium compound) are poured into a container. When an electric current is passed through the container, the negatively-charged oxygen particles in the alumina move to the positive anodes, while the positively-charged aluminium particles collect on the negative cathode floor, with a layer of liquid cryolite above. The pure aluminium can then be siphoned off.

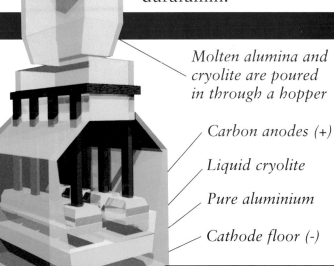

Molten alumina and cryolite are poured in through a hopper

Carbon anodes (+)

Liquid cryolite

Pure aluminium

Cathode floor (-)

POSTERS & PRINTING

Technological advances in printing had revolutionized advertizing. Before the 1850s, most posters had been typographic (with printed words only), and had the occasional wood-cut picture. They were printed in a single colour (usually black) and the design was extremely busy.

By the 1900s, the streets were plastered with pictorial posters printed in a riot of colours.

Peter Behrens designed this poster for a 1914 exhibition of Deutsche Werkbund products. The subtitle reads: 'Art in craft, industry and commerce • architecture.'

® LRT

Sans-serif typefaces suited the simpler, cleaner design look (a serif is a short stroke at the tip of a printed letter). The London Underground's typeface was designed in 1916 by Edward Johnston (1872–1944).

28

DEUTSCHE WERKBUND-
AUSSTELLUNG
KUNST IN HANDWERK,
INDUSTRIE UND HANDEL · ARCHITEKTUR
MAI CÖLN 1914 OCT.

THE SCIENCE OF PRINTING

All this colour was the result of the development during the 19th century of techniques for making multi-coloured prints first by hand – and then by machines through a process called offset lithography.

GETTING THE PRINTING PRESSES ROLLING

Lithography is based on the chemical principle that oil and water do not mix. In offset lithography, a flexible, metal printing plate is wrapped around a printing cylinder. A grease-based ink is rolled on to the printing cylinder, which is dampened by water rollers. The image to be printed accepts the greasy ink, but the damp, non-image areas reject it. The inked image is then 'offset' on to a rubber 'blanket' roller, and from there to a sheet or roll of paper.

One of the most prolific type designers of the 20th century was the American Frederic Goudy (1865–1947). Perhaps his most successful typeface was Goudy Old Style, designed in 1915.

1 2 3 4 5 6 7 8 9 0

A B C D E F G H I J K L M N O P Q R S T U V W X Y Z

Bovril will make a man of him

The other important advance in printing technology was the mechanization of typography. Before the invention of practical typesetting machines in the 1880s, every single letter in every single printed word had been hand set by a human typesetter. Colour lithography and mechanized typesetting meant that poster design could now be done by artists instead of by typesetters, and it was this that gave rise to the new style of poster.

THE ART OF POSTERS

Among the artists creating posters at the turn of the century were the French painter Henri de Toulouse-Lautrec (1864–1901), the Czech Alphonse Mucha, and the American Maxfield Parrish (1870–1966). A single striking image dominated these new-look posters. Words were kept to a minimum, and type was large and dramatic. The term 'graphic designer' (someone who specializes in drawing, printing and lettering) wasn't coined until the 1920s, but the role had emerged during the previous two decades.

Poster designs of the period ranged from the cool formality of Peter Behren's work, to the bold emotionalism of this 1914 poster by Artur Berger.

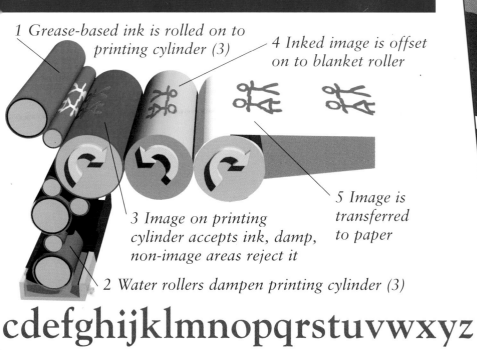

1 *Grease-based ink is rolled on to printing cylinder (3)*

4 *Inked image is offset on to blanket roller*

5 *Image is transferred to paper*

3 *Image on printing cylinder accepts ink, damp, non-image areas reject it*

2 *Water rollers dampen printing cylinder (3)*

cdefghijklmnopqrstuvwxyz

MARX

EMAIL

STREICHFERTIGE LACKE

GLOSSARY

ART NOUVEAU A decorative arts and architecture style of the 1880s–1900s, characterized by stylized plant and animal motifs and sinuous, curling patterns.

ASSEMBLY LINE A continuous series of machines and workers along which a product passes during its manufacture.

CAST IRON A form of iron suitable for casting – objects are made by pouring molten cast iron into moulds and allowing it to cool and solidify.

CUBISM A revolutionary artistic movement that developed in the early 20th century, which explored the non-realistic representation of objects as abstract, geometric shapes.

DEUTSCHE WERKBUND An association founded in Germany in 1907, with the aim of improving industrial products by forging closer ties between artists, industrialists and craftworkers.

DURALUMIN A strong, light alloy of about 94 per cent aluminium with other metals, developed in 1908–12.

INDUSTRIAL DESIGNER Someone who designs products that will be made by machines.

MASS-PRODUCTION The manufacture of standardized products in large quantities, usually by machines.

MODERNISM An international movement in architecture and design that emerged in the early 20th century. Rejecting historical styles and unnecessary decoration, modernists believed that the appearance of an object or building should be determined by its use.

REINFORCED CONCRETE Concrete strengthened by having steel bars or wires embedded in it.

STAINLESS STEEL An alloy of about 74 per cent steel with chromium and nickel, which was developed in 1912.

SUFFRAGETTE A woman who campaigned for voting rights in the early 20th century.

VIENNA WORKSHOPS An association of artists and craftworkers founded in Austria in 1903, to promote the manufacture of high-quality, handcrafted goods.

WROUGHT IRON A form of iron suitable for welding or working on a forge, which can be used to make ornamental ironwork, chains, bolts, and so on.

30

TIMELINE

	WORLD EVENTS	TECHNOLOGY	FAMOUS PEOPLE	ART & MEDIA
00	• Boxer Rising in China • UK Labour Party formed	• First vacuum cleaner patented by Hubert Booth	• Freud: The Interpretation of Dreams	• Puccini: Tosca • Beatrix Potter: Peter Rabbit
01	• Commonwealth of Australia proclaimed	• Marconi sends trans-atlantic morse code signal	• Death of Queen Victoria • President McKinley shot	• Chekhov: The Three Sisters • Rudyard Kipling: Kim
02	• South Africa: Second Boer War ends			• Georges Méliès's 14-minute film A Trip to the Moon
03	• UK: Women's Social and Political Union	• Wright brothers achieve first powered flight	• Henry Ford founds Ford Motor Company in Detroit	• Jack London: Call of the Wild
04	• Japan & Russia at war (to 1905)	• Autochrome colour films patented by Lumière brothers		• Joseph Conrad: Nostromo • Synge: Riders to the Sea
05	• Norway independent (of Sweden)		• Albert Einstein: Special Theory of Relativity	
06	• USA: San Francisco earthquake	• Enrico Forlanini tests first successful hydrofoil	• Theodore Roosevelt wins Nobel Peace Prize	
07	• New Zealand acquires Dominion status	• First synthetic plastic, Bakelite, invented		• Picasso: Les Demoiselles d'Avignon (first cubist art)
08	• Austria annexes Bosnia-Herzegovina	• Model T Ford launched • Hoover first marketed	• Baden-Powell founds the Boy Scout Movement	• Matisse: The Dinner Table (Harmony in Red)
09	• Young Turks overthrow Turkish Sultan		• Blériot flies across Channel • Russian Ballet visits Paris	• Strauss: Der Rosenkavalier
10	• Union of South Africa created	• Cellophane developed • First seaplane flown	• Death of Edward VII • Mother Teresa born	• Stravinsky: The Firebird • Kandinsky: Cossacks
11	• Chinese revolution: emperor overthrown	• First motorized washing machine	• Amundsen reaches the South Pole	
12	• Balkan Wars (to '13)	• Duralumin & stainless steel developed	• Robert Scott dies in Antarctica	• Ravel's Daphnis et Chloë first performed
13		• First geothermal power station opens, in Italy	• Suffragette Emily Davidson dies at the Derby	• Proust: Swann's Way
14	• Outbreak of World War I	• Traffic lights first installed, in the USA	• Assassination of Archduke Franz Ferdinand, Sarajevo	• Charlie Chaplin's tramp appears in Kid Auto Races
15	• ANZAC troops slaughtered on Gallipoli	• Chemical weapons first used in warfare	• Death of Rupert Brooke	• Malevich: Eight Red Rectangles
16	• Ireland: Easter Rising in Dublin	• Tanks first used in battle	• Margaret Sanger opens USA's 1st birth-control clinic	• D.W. Griffith: Intolerance • Kafka: Metamorphosis
17	• Russian Revolution • USA enters war	• Clarence Birdseye starts deep-freezing food	• Mata Hari executed as a spy	• Mary Pickford stars in Poor Little Rich Girl
18	• World War I ends • UK: women get vote		• Russian tsar & his family are murdered	• Sassoon: Counterattack • Woolf: Night and Day
19	• Treaty of Versailles • Nazi Party founded	• Ernest Rutherford splits the atom	• Alcock & Brown make first transatlantic flight	• Marcel Duchamp: Fountain

INDEX